MW01492853

Oxygen

Avery Elizabeth Hurt

Enslow Publishing
101 W. 23rd Street
Suite 240
New York, NY 10011
USA
enslow.com

Published in 2019 by Enslow Publishing, LLC.
101 W. 23rd Street, Suite 240, New York, NY 10011

Library of Congress Cataloging-in-Publication Data

Names: Hurt, Avery Elizabeth, author.
Title: Oxygen / Avery Elizabeth Hurt.
Description: New York, NY : Enslow Publishing, LLC, 2019. | Series: Exploring the elements | Audience: Grades 5 to 8. | Includes bibliographical references and index.
Identifiers: LCCN 2017051443 | ISBN 9780766099234 (library bound) | ISBN 9780766099241 (pbk.)
Subjects: LCSH: Oxygen—Juvenile literature. | Gases—Juvenile literature. | Chemical elements—Juvenile literature.
Classification: LCC QD181.01 H87 2019 | DDC 546/.721—dc23
LC record available at https://lccn.loc.gov/2017051443

Printed in the United States of America

To Our Readers: We have done our best to make sure all website addresses in this book were active and appropriate when we went to press. However, the author and the publisher have no control over and assume no liability for the material available on those websites or on any websites they may link to. Any comments or suggestions can be sent by email to customerservice@enslow.com.

Portions of this book appeared in *Oxygen* by Mary Thomas.

Photo Credits: Cover, p. 1 (chemical element symbols) Jason Winter/Shutterstock.com; cover, p. 1 (oxygen mask) Andrey_Popov/Shutterstock.com; p. 5 NASA/AFP/Getty Images; p. 8 Hulton Archive/Getty Images; p. 9 snapgalleria/Shutterstock.com; p. 11 LoopAll/Shutterstock.com; p. 14 Golden Sikorka/Shutterstock.com; p. 15 Designua/Shutterstock.com; p. 18 Richard Bizley/Science Source; p. 19 NNehring/E+/Getty Images; p. 20 NoPainNoGain/Shutterstock.com; p. 24 PM Images/The Image Bank/Getty Images; p. 27 Yakov Oskanov/Shutterstock.com; p. 30 madpixblue/Shutterstock.com; p. 33 udaix/Shutterstock.com; p. 34 Turtle Rock Scientific/Science Source; p. 36 islandboy_stocker/Shutterstock.com; p. 39 ellepigrafica/Shutterstock.com; p. 41 Prath/Shutterstock.com.

Contents

Introduction

//

On July 20, 1969, for the first time, humans stepped out of their spacecraft and walked on the surface of another heavenly body.

The Apollo mission to the Moon was one of the greatest scientific achievements of the twentieth century. Now, in the twenty-first century, humans are exploring Mars, but how will they breathe upon arrival?

As early as the 1960s and 1970s, the United States and the Soviet Union began studying Mars. In the 1960s, both nations sent spacecraft on "flybys" of Mars to take photographs and gather information from orbit. In 1965, NASA's *Mariner Four* got the first close-up images of Mars, and in 1971 the Soviets sent a lander to the surface of Mars. It crashed on landing, but a second attempt survived long enough to send back twenty seconds of useful video. From 1975 to 1980, two NASA orbiters and landers, *Viking*

One and *Viking Two*, mapped the Red Planet and searched for signs of life. In 1997, NASA placed the first-ever surface lander and the rover *Sojourner* on Mars. In 2003, the European Space Agency joined the exploration of Mars, sending landers and orbiters. In 2011, NASA sent *Curiosity*, the largest and most sophisticated exploration rover ever to visit another planet. *Curiosity* explored for two years and found evidence that liquid water had once existed on Mars.

On July 20, 1969, humans first set foot on the moon. The Apollo 11 mission to the moon was one of the greatest scientific achievements of the twentieth century.

But as exciting as these missions have been, no humans have visited Mars. That may change soon. In 2017, NASA outlined its plans to send a manned mission to the Red Planet by 2033. But plans for Mars are a great deal bigger than those for the moon. Scientists hope to one day colonize Mars. If people are going to live, work, and study on Mars, they are going to need something Mars doesn't have much of: oxygen.

The Martian atmosphere is 96 percent carbon dioxide and less than 2 percent oxygen. Getting humans to Mars is a big challenge.

Making sure they survive when they get there is an even bigger one, and so is being able to return home. Both surviving on Mars and getting back to Earth require oxygen.

NASA has a plan for that. The Mars Oxygen In-Situ Resource Utilization Experiment—called Moxie for short—is NASA's plan for producing oxygen from the atmosphere on Mars. A machine would use an electric current to separate the carbon and oxygen atoms that make up the carbon dioxide in the Martian atmosphere. The oxygen would then be available for astronauts to breathe and for firing the rockets that would send them back home.

The word "moxie" means bold—and this is definitely a bold plan. It's also a necessary one if humans are going to do more than make a quick visit to Mars. Humans cannot survive for more than a few minutes without oxygen.

But as important as it is to us now, Earth hasn't always had oxygen. And even after humans came along, it took a long time for us to understand what oxygen was. Once we did, we found a lot of ways to put it to use—including firing rockets to get to other planets.

1

Finding the Pieces

T ake a deep breath. Now, take another. Breathe slowly. Can you taste the oxygen in the air? Probably not because oxygen is tasteless, odorless, and colorless. You may not be able to see, taste, or touch oxygen, but it is absolutely essential to life in our world. Without it our planet might look more like Mars or the moon— dry and lifeless. There would be no clouds, rain, or snow because they each require water, and water is nearly 90 percent oxygen. (Hydrogen accounts for the remaining 10 percent.) Without oxygen, there would be none of the plants and animals that you see every day because oxygen is vital to nearly every organism on Earth.

Oxygen is an element. Elements are made of only one kind of substance that cannot be broken down further. The elements are the building blocks of life. If you imagine matter as a giant puzzle, the elements are the puzzle pieces—really, really small puzzle pieces. By fitting the "pieces" together in one way, you can create a grain of sand. Try a different combination, and you can create a drop of water, a rock, or even a person!

Scientists have discovered more than one hundred elements. Earth is about four and a half billion years old, but many of the elements were discovered only during the last few hundred years. Oxygen was "officially" discovered by two chemists working independently during the eighteenth century: Carl Scheele of Sweden and Joseph Priestly of England.

Carl Scheele of Sweden was one of two scientists to discover oxygen.

In 1773, Scheele discovered that whenever he heated nitric acid, a colorless liquid that can cause severe burns and is often used in fertilizer, a gas was released that made nearby candles burn brighter. Scheele wrote that the atmosphere was composed of two gases: one that supports combustion, or burning, which he called "fire air," and the other that prevents it, which he called "foul air."

A year or so later in England, Priestly discovered that the gas released by heating a mixture of mercury and air also made candles burn brighter. He published his findings in 1775, two years before Scheele, and took most of the credit for the discovery of what he called "dephlogisticated air." Another scientist, Antoine Lavoisier, gave oxygen its name and realized that it was an essential chemical element.

The Oxygen Puzzle

The puzzle pieces are called molecules. Molecules are made up of something even smaller: atoms. An atom is the smallest piece of an element that can unite with other atoms to form a molecule.

Subatomic Particles

Atoms are made up of tiny pieces called subatomic particles. These particles are protons, neutrons, and electrons. Protons have a positive electric charge, electrons have a negative electric charge, and neutrons have no charge at all. If you were to view an atom

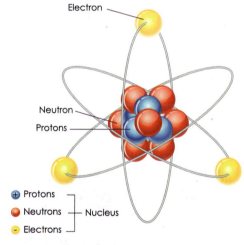

Electron

Neutron
Protons

⊕ Protons
● Neutrons — Nucleus
⊖ Electrons

Atoms are made up of tiny pieces called subatomic particles. These particles are protons, neutrons, and electrons.

Oxygen at a Glance

Chemical Symbol: O

Properties: Nonmetal, odorless, colorless, tasteless gas.

Discovered by: Independently by Joseph Priestly and Carl Scheele

Atomic Number: 8

Atomic Mass: 15.9994

Protons: 8

Electrons: 8

Neutrons: 8

Density: 1.429 kg/m^3

Melting Point: 54.36 K (-361.82 °F)

Boiling Point: 90.18 K (-297.08 °F)

Commonly Found: Everywhere

through a very powerful microscope, you would find it is mostly made up of empty space.

The protons and neutrons are in the center, or nucleus, of an atom. The nucleus is small and heavy compared to the rest of the atom. An element's atomic number is equal to the number of protons contained in its nucleus. An oxygen atom contains eight protons, so its atomic number is eight. Another important property of an element is its atomic mass (or atomic weight). The atomic mass is the average sum of the number of protons and neutrons in each atom of the element. Electrons are light and do not really add to the weight. Ordinary oxygen has an atomic weight of 15.9994.

Outside the nucleus are the shells that contain the electrons. The first shell of an atom can hold only two electrons, the second shell can hold up to eight, and the third shell can hold more than eight. The oxygen atom has only two shells of electrons.

The inner shell contains two electrons. The outer shell contains six electrons.

The way the electrons are arranged in the atom influences how the atom behaves. An atom is the most stable when its electron shells are completely full (with two electrons in the first shell, eight in the second, and so forth). Knowing that oxygen has an atomic number of 8, we also know that it has eight protons and eight electrons. Because it has only six electrons in its outer shell, oxygen is always on the lookout for two more electrons to complete its outer electron shell. This means that oxygen is highly reactive—very likely to combine with other elements. When oxygen combines with two hydrogen molecules, it forms what is probably Earth's most important compound: water.

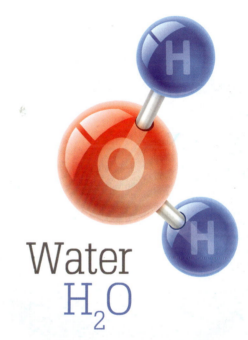

Water
H_2O

When oxygen combines with two hydrogen molecules, it forms what is probably Earth's most important compound: water.

Changing Characters

Oxygen's particular combination of subatomic particles makes it different from other elements in the periodic table. If we were able to take away a proton from oxygen so that it had seven protons, it would be a totally different element—nitrogen (N). If we added a proton, giving it nine protons, it would become another element— fluorine (F). The number of protons in the nucleus of an atom determines what element it is.

Oxygen's makeup of protons, neutrons and electrons makes it able to bond, or join, very easily with other elements to form compounds. This is one of the reasons oxygen and oxygen compounds are so common in our universe.

2

Arranging Families: The Periodic Table

ith so many elements to keep track of, scientists began to look for ways to organize them all. In 1870, a Russian chemist and professor at the University of St. Petersburg, Dmitry Ivanovich Mendeleev, created a special chart to help his students remember the elements. He placed the elements in horizontal rows according to their atomic mass. The lightest element was placed at the left and the heaviest at the right. He called this the periodic table.

PERIODIC TABLE OR MENDELEEV'S TABLE

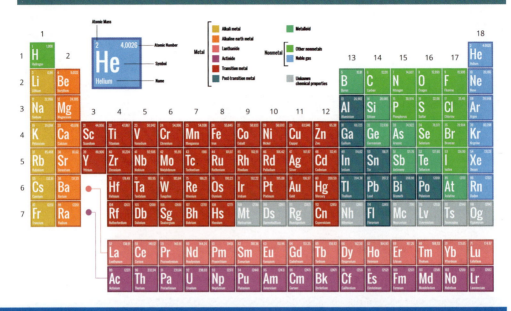

In 1870, Russian chemist and professor Dmitry Ivanovich Mendeleev created a special chart to help his students remember the elements.

The table allowed scientists to see for the first time the relationships, trends, and patterns between elements. These relationships and trends are called properties. Properties can be the color, taste, smell, and chemical behavior of an element.

Today, the periodic table still uses Mendeleev's arrangement of the elements according to their atomic mass. The elements are also organized into groups numbered 1 through 18. The number of the group appears above each column of the table. In the same way that members of the same family often resemble one another, elements within these groups also have similar chemical properties. In fact, these groups are often referred to as "families" of elements. By arranging the elements this way, scientists could predict whether any given element was a metal, a nonmetal, or a metalloid, an element that has the properties of both a metal and a nonmetal.

The Properties of Oxygen

In addition to color, taste, smell, and chemical behavior, another property of an element is its physical state when at room temperature. All elements can appear in one of three physical states: solid, liquid, or gas.

STATES OF MATTER

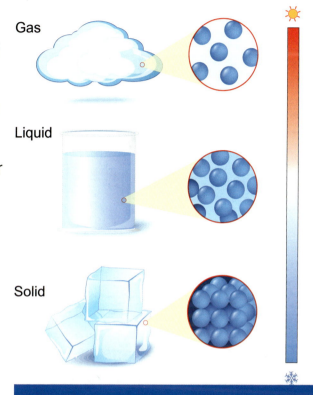

Gas

Liquid

Solid

When at room temperature, all elements can appear in one of three physical states: solid, liquid, or gas.

At room temperature, oxygen is a gas. When cooled to -360° Fahrenheit (-218° C)—far colder than anything that occurs naturally on Earth—oxygen becomes a solid. Oxygen's boiling point is higher than other elements in the air, which makes it possible to extract

Oxygen's Place at the Table

Oxygen (chemical symbol O) is located within Group VI on the periodic table. Group VI also contains sulfur (S), selenium (Se), tellurium (Te), and polonium (Po). The elements are divided by a "staircase line" that extends from boron (B) to astatine, chemical symbol (At) on the lower right portion of the periodic table. This staircase line separates the metals from the nonmetals. Metals, like potassium (K), sodium, (Na), and iron (Fe) are located to the left of this line. The nonmetals, such as chlorine (C) and nitrogen (N), are located to the right of the line. Oxygen is located on the right side of the staircase line with the other nonmetals.

oxygen from air by a cooling process that involves alternately compressing and expanding air in pressure-sealed containers. When the air temperature is cooled to nearly -330° F (-201°C), oxygen becomes a liquid. It can then be distilled and stored as a liquid in metal pressurized containers. Liquid oxygen can be contained and moved by using a strong magnet.

3

Oxygen and Our World

You might say that elements are the substances that make the universe tick. Oxygen is definitely the element that makes life on Earth tick. Oxygen is not the most abundant element, but it does take up the most space on Earth. It makes up nearly half of our planet's bulk, or mass. Every 100 pounds of soil contains about 47 pounds of oxygen.

It's a good thing, too. The weather would be pretty rough in an oxygen-free world. Without oxygen, the atmosphere—the mass of air that surrounds Earth like a blanket—would be much thinner, for starters. Scientists believe that with far less atmosphere to protect Earth's surface from solar radiation and no clouds to help trap the sun's warmth, Earth's weather might more closely resemble that of

Scientists believe Earth started out as little more than a big rock surrounded by a cloud of gases harmful to the people, plants, and animal life that live here now.

Mars: windy, with fierce dust storms and low temperatures. Imagine a world where the average temperature on a sunny day is about -10° F (23° C). Without oxygen, Earth wouldn't be a nice place to live at all.

The Elixir of Life

Oxygen wasn't always so important. Until just a few billion years ago, there wasn't much oxygen on Earth at all. Scientists believe that Earth started out as little more than a big rock surrounded by a cloud of gases that would be harmful to people, plants, and animal life that live here now. These gases included methane, hydrogen, and ammonia.

A combination of substances in the rock and increasing pressure very slowly built up enough heat to melt the interior of Earth. The heavier materials, such as iron, sank toward the middle of this "Earth soup," while lighter silicates, or rocks made of silicon and oxygen, rose to the surface to form Earth's earliest crust.

The Oxygen Apocalypse

When oxygen first appeared in Earth's atmosphere, it was a disaster for the life that lived there. There weren't any plants or animals, but the ocean was teeming with bacteria. Bacteria are very simple life

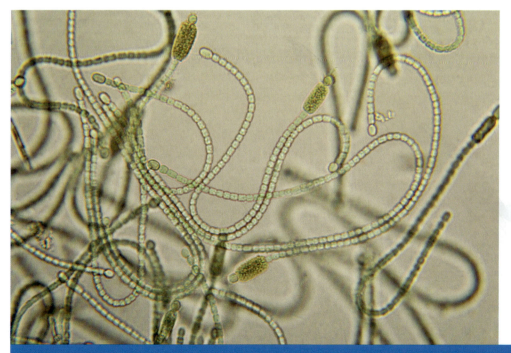

Cyanobacteria were different than any other life form that came before. Like plants do today, they used photosynthesis to change sunlight into food.

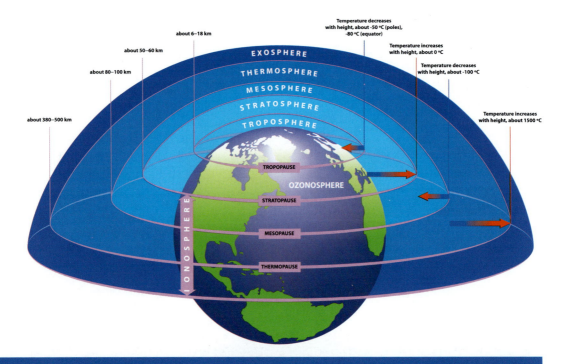

Temperature decreases with height, about -50 °C (poles), -80 °C (equator)

Temperature increases with height, about 0 °C

Temperature decreases with height, about -100 °C

Temperature increases with height, about 1500 °C

about 6–18 km

about 50–60 km

about 80–100 km

about 380–500 km

EXOSPHERE

THERMOSPHERE

MESOSPHERE

STRATOSPHERE

TROPOSPHERE

TROPOPAUSE

OZONOSPHERE

STRATOPAUSE

MESOPAUSE

THERMOPAUSE

IONOSPHERE

Earth's atmosphere is made of different layers: the troposphere, the stratosphere, the mesosphere, the thermosphere, and the exosphere.

forms. The bacteria that lived on Earth at this time were anaerobic bacteria, meaning they did not need oxygen to survive. In fact, oxygen was poisonous to them. Then about two and a half billion years ago, a new type of life evolved. This new life was cyanobacteria—also known as blue-green algae. Cyanobacteria were different. Like plants do today, they used photosynthesis to change sunlight into food.

The light used in photosynthesis is absorbed by a green pigment, called chlorophyll, within each food-making cell. The sunlight causes water to split into molecules of hydrogen and oxygen. The hydrogen combines with carbon dioxide from the air, forming a simple sugar. Oxygen from the water molecules is given off in the process. As far as the anaerobic bacteria were concerned, the new bacteria were exhaling poison. Eventually, so much oxygen built up on the planet that the anaerobic bacteria in the ocean died off in what is called a mass extinction. Scientists call this the Great Oxygen Event. But what was a disaster for anaerobic bacteria was good for the more complex life forms—including people—that were to come.

Oxygen in the Air

Even before people knew what oxygen was, they knew it was important to life. Throughout history, especially before the eighteenth century when oxygen was discovered, many people thought that air was made of only one substance. As you will see, the study of oxygen is closely linked to the study of air. Most people use the two words interchangeably even today. But in truth, they are quite different.

Air is more accurately called atmosphere. It covers our whole planet and extends far above its surface. Air is invisible and has no taste or smell. Yet, it is as real as anything you can see, taste, or touch. This atmosphere—the air we breathe—is actually a finely tuned mixture of gases. Oxygen makes up about 20 percent of that mixture. The remaining 80 percent of the air is a combination of several other gases.

The Air Up There

Here is a closer look at the special ingredients that make up our atmosphere.

Gas	Percentage by Volume
Nitrogen	78.084
Oxygen	20.946
Argon	0.934
Neon	0.0018
Helium	0.000524
Methane	0.0002
Krypton	0.000114
Hydrogen	0.00005
Nitrous oxide	0.00005
Xenon	0.0000087

A molecule that contains three oxygen atoms is called ozone. In the upper layers of the atmosphere, ozone helps protect Earth from harmful ultraviolet rays from the sun. Close to the ground, however, ozone is not so helpful. It is the main component of smog and can cause serious damage to your lungs. Ground-level ozone is produced by reactions involving chemicals called hydrocarbons and nitrogen oxides in the presence of sunlight.

Scientists are concerned because smog and other forms of pollution have been proven to damage the ozone layer (the helpful one, up high). Without its protection, the sun's rays can damage plants and the eyes and skin of animals, including people.

4

What Fire Breathes: Oxygen and Combustion

//

Though we depend on it for life, oxygen can be destructive. One of oxygen's most destructive, yet important, roles in our world is combustion, or burning. When something burns, it reacts with oxygen to create light, heat, and energy in the form of fire.

Millions of years ago, people were both frightened and fascinated by the warmth, beauty, and power of fire. And rightly so. Fire keeps people warm and allows them to cook food. It's also very dangerous. A fire that gets out of control could destroy everything in its path.

One of oxygen's most destructive, yet important, roles in our world is combustion, or burning.

Humans have known about combustion for thousands of years, but we have made little progress in controlling fire.

Fire is neither a solid nor a liquid. To ancient people, fire seemed more like the wind, except that it was hot and bright and could do just about whatever it wanted. Ancient people believed fire was magical, and many cultures worshipped it. Even cultures that didn't worship fire thought it was essential to life.

From Yin and Yang to Oxygen and Nitrogen

Philosophers and physicians of the ancient world tried to understand fire. Anaximenes, a Greek philosopher, argued that the world developed out of air as early as 545 BCE. He believed that air turned into other things, like water and earth, through something like condensation, a process by which a substance is changed into a denser form. According to Anaximenes, through condensation air becomes visible, first as a mist or cloud, then as water, and finally as solid matter like rocks. Eventually, he thought, it turns to fire.

In about 450 BCE Empedocles, another Greek philosopher, discovered that when he tried to lower an empty container upside-down into a barrel of water, it was difficult to get the water to go inside. Empedocles thought that something was taking up the space within the container, preventing the water from going inside. To test his idea, he cut a small hole into the bottom of the container and tried his experiment again. This time, the water filled the inside of the container quickly and easily. Whatever had been inside had escaped through the hole in the bottom. Empedocles quickly figured out that this invisible substance must be air.

Empedocles came to believe that air must be one of the basic elements from which all matter is created. The other elements were earth, fire, and water. He also believed that nothing in the universe can be created or destroyed, only transformed into other objects depending on different combinations of those four essential ingredients. He may have been wrong about some of the details, but he was definitely on the right track.

In 8 CE, a Chinese alchemist named Mao-Khóa is said to have believed that the atmosphere is composed of two invisible components called *yin* and *yang*. Like philosophers, alchemists were among the world's first scientists. Alchemists usually combined religion, philosophy, and chemistry for three main aims: to transform metals like copper and lead into precious silver and gold, to cure disease, and to extend life. Many alchemy experiments were designed to uncover the "Elixir of Life" that they believed would lead to eternal health and immortality.

According to Mao-Khóa, yin was "incomplete air" that bonded easily with many substances. By heating charcoal or saltpetre, a substance often used in gunpowder, yin is removed from the air, making it more perfect. Mao-Khóa believed that yang was "complete air." While there is no evidence today of his experiments, Mao-Khóa was almost certainly on a path to discovery that European scientists would complete hundreds of years later. When they realized that air wasn't a single element at all but a mixture of gases, European scientists would give new names—oxygen and nitrogen—to what Mao-Khóa had called yin and yang.

One of the first people to catch on to the idea that the air was actually a mixture of gases was Leonardo da Vinci. He wrote, "Where flame cannot live, no animal that draws breath can live." Leonardo was an Italian painter and sculptor who lived during the late fifteenth century. His paintings the *Mona Lisa* and *The Last*

Supper are among the most popular and influential paintings of the Renaissance era. Leonardo was also a great engineer and scientist. He observed that a fire needed the air around it in order to burn. He carefully watched the air being taken into the body with every breath as a candle burned nearby. He realized that it was impossible for air to be an element because it was obviously composed of different parts. Finally, a breath of fresh air!

Phlogiston: The Wrong Road

By the start of the eighteenth century, scientists had different ideas about air and fire. They had figured out that the universe was made of more than water, air, fire, and earth. German chemist and physician Georg Ernst Stahl came to believe that anything that

Fire, scientists used to think, was caused by the release of phlogiston into the air. The word "phlogiston" comes from Greek, meaning "burned."

could burn was in part composed of a substance called phlogiston. Fire, he reasoned, was caused by the release of this substance into the air. The word "phlogiston" comes from Greek, meaning "burned."

Stahl believed that air was very important for combustion because it absorbed the phlogiston as it was released. Plants helped remove the substance from the air by absorbing it, and therefore the plants burned when they were dry. Stahl also believed that the corrosion of metals exposed to air, such as the rusting of iron, was a form of combustion. When a metal was converted to its calx, or metallic ash (oxide, in modern terms), phlogiston was lost. Therefore, metals were composed of calx and phlogiston. Like all other good chemical theories, the phlogiston theory offered an explanation for the results of a variety of experiments and suggested clues to other scientific puzzles. For that reason, the theory was widely accepted in the 1700s and led to many findings in chemistry.

The major objection to this theory was that the ash of organic substances, such as wood, often weighed less than the original substance. But the calx was heavier than the metal. Stahl thought of phlogiston more as an immaterial "principle" than as an actual substance, however. As the study of chemistry advanced, phlogiston was considered a true substance, and many scientists worked to account for the weight changes. When hydrogen, a very light and extremely flammable element, was discovered, some thought it was pure phlogiston.

One of the scientists who studied these weight differences was a French chemist named Antoine Lavoisier. During his own experiments with fire, he realized that Scheele's "fire air," which Priestly had named "dephlogisticated air," helped the calx gain weight by chemically combining with some of the air around it, not because it absorbed phlogiston. Later, he noticed that this same "fire air" tended to form acids when mixed with certain substances. From the Greek words *oxys*, meaning "acid," and *genos*, meaning "forming," Lavoisier renamed the gas oxygen. Many chemists first rejected Lavoisier's findings and tried to retain some form of the phlogiston theory, but by 1800 practically every chemist accepted Lavoisier's oxygen theory.

Fighting Fire

Firefighters control and put out fires. One of the ways they do this is by limiting the supply of oxygen available to the fire. Sometimes they spray the fire with a mist of water from fog nozzles on their hoses. Millions of small particles of water fill up the air space that might have been used by oxygen. Firefighters can also spray foam from a fire extinguisher on the fire. They may also use specially made blankets that do not burn to smother the fire. The idea behind all of these methods of fighting fires is to deny the fire the oxygen it needs to burn.

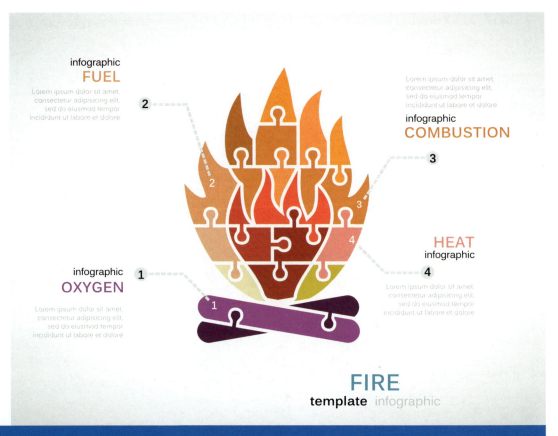

infographic
FUEL
Lorem ipsum dolor sit amet, consectetur adipisicing elit, sed do eiusmod tempor incididunt ut labore et dolore

Lorem ipsum dolor sit amet, consectetur adipisicing elit, sed do eiusmod tempor incididunt ut labore et dolore

infographic
COMBUSTION

infographic
OXYGEN
Lorem ipsum dolor sit amet, consectetur adipisicing elit, sed do eiusmod tempor incididunt ut labore et dolore

HEAT
infographic
Lorem ipsum dolor sit amet, consectetur adipisicing elit, sed do eiusmod tempor incididunt ut labore et dolore

FIRE
template infographic

Scientists define combustion as an exothermic reaction—a chemical reaction that creates heat and light. It is a form of oxidation that takes place between a fuel and a gas.

Combustion and Our World

Today, combustion helps generate electricity and provides the power for car and train engines, airplanes, and even spacecraft. Scientists define combustion as an exothermic reaction—a chemical reaction that creates heat and light. It is a form of oxidation that takes place between a fuel and a gas. A fuel can be anything that burns, like wood or coal. The gas is usually oxygen from the air, although other gases, like chlorine, may also be involved.

Fire is a chemical process. Three things are needed for fire: oxygen, heat, and fuel. A fire cannot start or continue if even one of these elements is missing. During this chemical process, the molecules within oxygen and the fuel rearrange themselves. Energy is either released or absorbed. The process in a fire is called oxidation, where oxygen atoms combine with hydrogen and carbon to form water and carbon dioxide.

Fuels burn only when they have been heated to a certain point, called the ignition temperature. The heat, usually from a match or spark, is just enough heat to turn some of the fuel into a gas, providing a sort of "kick start" to the burning process.

Oxidation is the same chemical process that turns iron into rust. But with iron, the reaction is very slow, and the heat energy that is released is very low. With certain things, like paper or wood, the oxidation rate of the molecules can be very fast. If the heat cannot be released faster than it is created, then flames are created.

5

Oxides: Oxygen Makes Friends

//

Elements combine to form compounds, or combinations of elements. In chemistry, a compound is a substance formed from two or more elements.

Water is a compound made out of hydrogen and oxygen—two hydrogen atoms for every one oxygen atom. This is expressed as the chemical formula H_2O.

Because oxygen is one of the most reactive elements, it combines easily with other elements. Almost every element, except helium (He), neon (Ne), Argon (Ar), Krypton (Kr), and Fluorine (F), can be found combined with oxygen. If you look at the periodic table, you'll see that most of these elements are within Group VIII and are called inert gases. The name "inert" means an element is not

Elements, Compounds and Mixtures

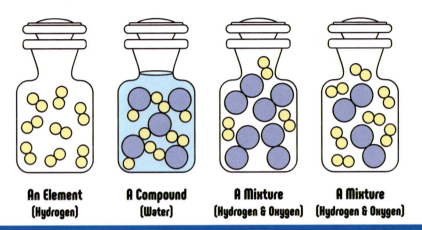

| An Element (Hydrogen) | A Compound (Water) | A Mixture (Hydrogen & Oxygen) | A Mixture (Hydrogen & Oxygen) |

Elements combine to form compounds, or combinations of elements. In chemistry, a compound is a substance formed from two or more elements.

chemically active. It's not just oxygen they shun; they rarely react with anything at all.

Oxides

Compounds of oxygen are called oxides. As Antoine Lavoisier realized, oxides are often made by heating or burning an element or a compound in the presence of air or oxygen.

Metal Oxides

When metals combine with oxygen, they form metal oxides, usually in the form of solid crystals. Magnesium oxide, for example, is white crystals, often mixed with magnesium chloride to form "stucco," a light-colored cement often used to decorate buildings.

Metal oxides usually occur through the process of ionic bonding. That's when the atoms of one element donate negatively charged electrons in their outer shells to the atoms of another element. In doing so, they become positively charged ions. In the case of metal oxides, the metal atoms donate electrons to oxygen atoms. The metal atom combines with an oxygen atom to form a compound. The resulting difference in electrical charge—the metal atoms have become positively charged ions, while the

Metal oxides occur through the process of ionic bonding, when the atoms of one element donate negatively charged electrons in their outer shells to the atoms of another element.

oxygen atoms have become negatively charged ions—causes the elements to bond together.

Nonmetal Oxides

Nonmetals combine differently with oxygen, choosing to share electrons rather than donating them to create nonmetal oxides. This process of sharing electrons is called covalent bonding, and this type of bond creates a molecule. Nonmetal oxides are usually very reactive and tend to form strong acids when dissolved in water. Their reactions are probably what Lavoisier observed when he coined the term oxygen, or "acid-former."

Oxidation

Oxygen is involved in two important processes: oxidation and reduction. These processes are used in many everyday activities, from burning fuels to helping plants and animals breathe, grow, and move. Originally, scientists used the term "oxidation" to

The Breathalyzer

A breathalyzer is a device that determines how much alcohol a person has consumed. Consuming too much alcohol impairs a person's ability to drive safely and puts that person and others at risk. Police use breathalyzers to tell when someone has had too much alcohol to drive safely. The breathalyzer contains chemicals that react with ethanol (the alcohol in alcoholic drinks) via an oxidation-reduction reaction. The ethanol is oxidized, while one of the other chemicals (potassium dichromate) is reduced. By measuring the products of this reaction, a breathalyzer determines how much alcohol a person has consumed.

When exposed to air, most metals oxidize, forming a dull metal oxide coating or tarnish. We call this rust.

mean that a substance was gaining oxygen. The term "reduction" meant that a substance was losing oxygen.

Today, scientists use the terms "oxidation" and "reduction" to describe any reaction that involves the transfer of electrons, even when oxygen is not involved. Atoms that lose electrons are said to be oxidized, and atoms that gain electrons are said to be reduced. Any substance or compound that donates oxygen or electrons, or accepts hydrogen to cause oxidation, is called an oxidizing agent.

Any substance that donates electrons to cause reduction is called a reducing agent.

Rust

Rusting is an oxidation process. When exposed to air, most metals oxidize, forming a dull metal oxide coating or tarnish. In the case of aluminum or silver, this coating protects the untarnished metal below it from the air and further corrosion. However, when iron and steel are exposed to oxygen, a layer of brown iron oxide forms on the surface of the metal. This layer does not protect the metal below it from air and moisture. It merely crumbles away, and the rust can quickly "eat" through the metal. The only way to protect against this process is to apply a protective coating that seals the metal from air and moisture.

6

Oxygen and Life

Oxygen is involved all life processes, such as breathing, moving, and digesting food. Here, too, the process of combustion plays an important role: it provides energy to your body. Scientists have coined a special term for this "slow burn" process. It is called cellular respiration.

During digestion, nutrients are turned into a chemical called glucose and carried to cells throughout the body. Glucose is a type of sugar. With help from oxygen, cells burn glucose. This provides energy for important life functions. During this process, the hydrogen within the glucose combines with the oxygen to make water, which is absorbed by your body. Glucose also contains carbon. Carbon combines with oxygen to create carbon dioxide, which cannot be used by the body. Carbon dioxide is removed from the body when you exhale, or breathe out.

When you breathe in, or inhale, you take oxygen from the air into your lungs. Each lung is lined with thousands of tiny passages, which are covered with even tinier blood vessels. Oxygen from the air seeps through the walls of these blood vessels into the blood. Red blood cells carry oxygen to all parts of your body. Oxygen is essential to all living tissue because it plays a role in the chemical processes important to life. A special substance called hemoglobin helps deliver oxygen to living tissue. Hemoglobin also helps take the carbon dioxide back to your lungs, where it can be exhaled.

This complex process is part of another, larger process called the oxygen cycle. This is a constant exchange of air and oxygen between animals and plants. Animals, including humans, inhale

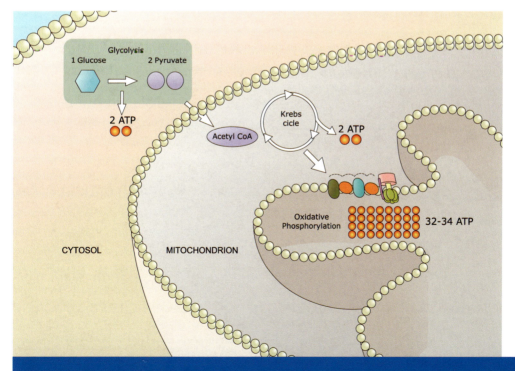

Cellular respiration involves combustion, too; this release of energy helps you breathe, digest food, and move.

oxygen from the air and exhale carbon dioxide. Plants absorb the carbon dioxide and release more oxygen into the air through photosynthesis. Photosynthesis is how plants create food. Without plants, humans and animals wouldn't be able to breathe. Without us breathing, plants wouldn't be able to produce oxygen. And without oxygen, there would be no life on Earth!

Oxygen at Work

Although oxygen is a naturally occurring element, it is often produced for use in many industries. These forms of oxygen can be found all around you.

Oxygen and Steel

Oxygen is also used to create steel. Workers use a blast of oxygen to remove dirt from the molten steel before other metals are added to create the finished steel product. The world's steel industry is by far the largest user of commercially produced oxygen. However, many kinds of welding and cutting tools use oxygen to create the super hot temperatures often necessary to cut and mold iron, steel, and other hard metals.

Oxygen is used in the medical industry as well. Doctors give oxygen to patients whose bodies are not strong enough to take it from the air and to treat patients who are suffering from carbon monoxide poisoning. Patients are given pure oxygen that goes

Oxygen in a Bottle

When it is chilled to -297° F (-183° C), air becomes liquid. Oxygen can be distilled from liquid air, compressed, and put into metal tanks, sometimes called oxygen bottles. Firefighters carry oxygen tanks and gas masks so that they can breathe inside burning buildings, where most of the oxygen is feeding the fire, or in other places where there is not enough air or the air is dangerous to breathe. Bottled oxygen is also used by climbers who travel to the highest mountain peaks, where the air is thin and oxygen is scarce. Divers also carry oxygen tanks to help them stay underwater for long periods of time.

Firefighters carry oxygen tanks so they can breathe inside burning buildings, where most of the free oxygen is feeding the fire.

right into their bloodstream. Oxygen is sometimes used to kill dangerous bacteria.

It's easy to take oxygen for granted because it is always around us, keeping us alive, yet we cannot see it, taste it, or smell it. But it is it always there. Oxygen's ability to combine with nearly every other element, as well as its ability to foster combustion, is responsible for a lot of what goes on inside people and other living things, not to mention what goes on in cars and furnaces.

Oxygen is the one thing that you absolutely, positively cannot do without, even for a minute, if you want to live. In the end, oxygen really is the "elixir of life" in our world.

Glossary

anaerobic Not needing or involving oxygen.

apocalypse Catastrophic destruction.

atmosphere The mixture of gases that covers the surface of the entire planet.

atom The smallest part of an element.

atomic number The number of protons that exist within the nucleus of an atom.

combustion Burning.

covalent Chemical bonds formed by sharing electrons.

electron Negatively charged particles found within atoms, but outside of the nucleus.

isotopes Atoms of a chemical element with the same atomic number and nearly identical chemical behavior but with differing atomic weights and different physical properties.

molecule A particle formed by two or more atoms bonded together

neutrons Atomic particles that have no electrical charge. Like protons, neutrons are found inside the nucleus.

nucleus The center region of an atom that contains protons and neutrons.

oxidation The process by which oxygen is added to something, or by which atoms donate electrons.

photosynthesis The method used by plants to make food energy.

protons Atomic particles that have a positive electrical charge. They are found inside of the nucleus.

reduction The process by which oxygen is removed from something, or by which atoms gain electrons.

Further Reading

Books

Johnson, Rose. *Discoveries in Chemistry That Changed the World*. New York, NY: Rosen Central, 2015.

Kean, Sam. *The Disappearing Spoon: And Other True Tales of Rivalry, Adventure, and the History of the World from the Periodic Table of the Elements* (Young Readers Edition). New York, NY: Little Brown, 2018.

Rich, Mari. *Oxygen* (The Chemistry of Everyday Elements) Broomall, PA: Mason Crest, 2017.

Stefoff, Rebecaa. *Alchemy and Chemistry*. New York, NY: Cavendish Square, 2014.

Websites

Elements for Kids

www.ducksters.com/science/chemistry/oxygen.php

Explore the element of oxygen

Kids Fun Science

www.kids-fun-science.com/plant-experiments.html

Create oxygen right at home!

Science for Kids Club

www.scienceforkidsclub.com/oxygen.html

Explore oxygen and do an experiment!

Bibliography

Atkins, P. W. *Periodic Kingdom*. New York, NY: Basic, 1995.

Elmsley, John. *Nature's Building Blocks: An A-Z Guide to the Elements.* New York, NY. Oxford University Press, 2003.

Elmsley, John. *Molecules at an Exhibition.* Los Angeles, CA: Getty Center for Education in the Arts, 1999.

Essential Chemical Industry. "Oxygen, Nitrogen, and the Rare Gases." http://www.essentialchemicalindustry.org/chemicals/oxygen.html. Accessed October 2017.

Gray, Theodore. *Elements: A Visual Exploration of Every Known Atom in the Universe.* New York, NY: Black Dog and Leventhal, 2012.

Gray, Theodore. *Molecules: The Elements and the Architecture of Everything.* New York, NY: Black Dog and Leventhal, 2014.

Heiserman, David L. *Exploring Chemical Elements and their Compounds.* New York, NY: McGraw-Hill Trade, 1991.

Lane, Nick. *Oxygen: The Molecule That Made the World.* New York, NY: Oxford University Press, 2002.

LeMay, H. Eugene. *Chemistry: Connections to Our Changing World.* Englewood Cliffs, NJ: Prentice Hall, 2000.

NASA. "Mars 2020 Rover." https://mars.nasa.gov/mars2020/mission/instruments/moxie/. Accessed October 2017.

NASA. "Mars Exploration Program." https://mars.nasa.gov. Accessed October 2017.

Royal Society of Chemistry. "Periodic Table (Oxygen)." http://www.rsc.org/periodic-table/element/8/oxygen. Accessed September 2017.

Scerri, Eric R. *The Periodic Table: A Very Short Introduction*. Oxford, UK: Oxford UP, 2011.

Science Shorts. "The Discovery of Oxygen." http://www.scienceshorts.com/the-discovery-of-oxygen/. Accessed September 2017.

Stwertka , Albert. *A Guide to the Elements*. New York, NY: Oxford University Press Children's Books, 1999.

Index